W9-CAH-195

4/24

TRIBES of NATIVE AMERICA

Narragansett

edited by Marla Felkins Ryan
and Linda Schmittroth

22266

BLACKBIRCH®
PRESS

THOMSON
GALE

San Diego • Detroit • New York • San Francisco • Cleveland
New Haven, Conn. • Waterville, Maine • London • Munich

THOMSON

GALE

© 2003 by Blackbirch Press™. Blackbirch Press™ is an imprint of The Gale Group, Inc., a division of Thomson Learning, Inc.

Blackbirch Press™ and Thomson Learning™ are trademarks used herein under license.

For more information, contact
The Gale Group, Inc.
27500 Drake Rd.
Farmington Hills, MI 48331-3535
Or you can visit our Internet site at http://www.gale.com

ALL RIGHTS RESERVED
No part of this work covered by the copyright hereon may be reproduced or used in any form or by any means—graphic, electronic, or mechanical, including photocopying, recording, taping, Web distribution or information storage retrieval systems—without the written permission of the publisher.

Every effort has been made to trace the owners of copyrighted material.

Photo credits: Cover Courtesy of Northwestern University Library; cover © National Archives; cover © Photospin; cover © Perry Jasper Photography; cover © Picturequest; cover © Seattle Post-Intelligencer Collection, Museum of History & Industry; cover, page 22 © PhotoDisc; cover, page 7 © Library of Congress; page 3, 20 © Courtesy the Rhode Island Historical Society. Annual Tribal Pow-wow of Narragansett Indians. August 9, 1925. Glass Plate Negative. Avery Lord. RHi L866 292; pages 5, 17, 27, 28 © AP WideWorld; pages 6, 14, 25 © CORBIS; pages 8, 9, 10, 11, 13, 29, 30 © North Wind Picture Archives; page 15 © Courtesy the Rhode Island Historical Society. Marks of the Sachems of the Narragansett Indians, Marks of 1644 of Pessacus, Canonicus, Mixanno, and Canonicus. RHi X3 6134; page 19 © Carnegie Abbey Club, Portsmouth, Rhode Island; page 20 © Courtesy the Rhode Island Historical Society. Gathering of the Narragansetts at the annual Pow Wow. August 9, 1925. Glass Plate Negative. Avery Lord. RHi X3 2466; page 23 © Hulton Archive

LIBRARY OF CONGRESS CATALOGING-IN-PUBLICATION DATA

Narragansett / Marla Felkins Ryan, book editor; Linda Schmittroth, book editor.
    v. cm. — (Tribes of Native America)
Includes bibliographical references.
Contents: Narragansett name — Origins and group affiliations — History — Language — Daily life — Customs — Current tribal issues.
  ISBN 1-56711-698-1 (alk. paper)
  1. Narragansett Indians—Juvenile literature. [1. Narragansett Indians. 2. Indians of North America—Rhode Island.] I. Ryan, Marla Felkins. II. Schmittroth, Linda. III. Series.

E99.N16 .N37 2003
974.5004'973—dc21   2002015828

Printed in United States
10 9 8 7 6 5 4 3 2 1

Table of Contents

NARRAGANSETT

Name

The name Narragansett (pronounced *nah-ruh-GAN-sit*) is used for both the people and the place where they lived. It may mean "people of the little points and bays." Today, the name is used for living members of the Eastern Niantic and Narragansett tribes.

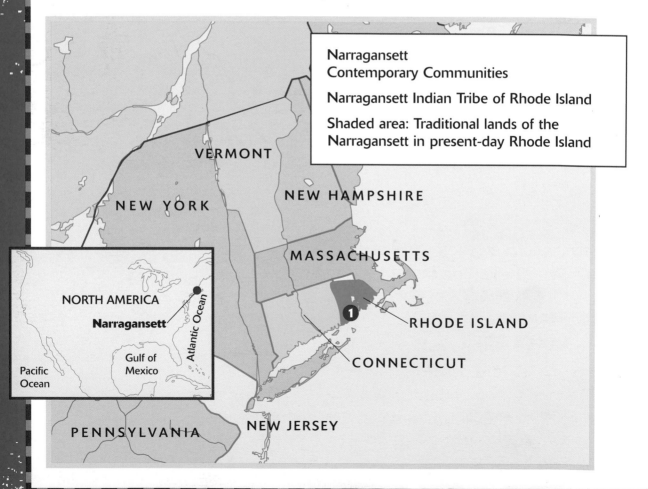

Narragansett
Contemporary Communities

Narragansett Indian Tribe of Rhode Island

Shaded area: Traditional lands of the Narragansett in present-day Rhode Island

VERMONT

NEW HAMPSHIRE

NEW YORK

MASSACHUSETTS

NORTH AMERICA

Narragansett

Atlantic Ocean

Gulf of Mexico

Pacific Ocean

RHODE ISLAND

CONNECTICUT

PENNSYLVANIA

NEW JERSEY

Where are the traditional Narragansett lands?

At the time when they were most powerful, the Narragansett lived on lands that made up most of what is now Rhode Island. They lived mainly on the Atlantic Coast and in the valleys and forests west of Narragansett Bay. Today, the Narragansett tribe owns a 1,943-acre reservation 45 miles south of Providence, Rhode Island. By the mid-1990s, no one lived on the reservation anymore. Most members of the Narragansett tribe lived in Rhode Island and Massachusetts.

The name Narragansett describes the Eastern Niantic and Narragansett tribes.

What has happened to the population?

In 1600, there were between 4,000 and 30,000 Narragansett. In a 1990 count of the population by the U.S. Census Bureau, 2,564 people said they were Narragansett.

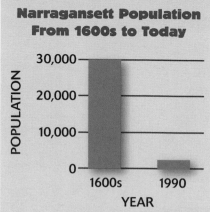

Narragansett Population From 1600s to Today

Origins and group ties

The Narragansett are one of the oldest Indian tribes in North America. They have been around since about 11,000 years ago. Powerful Narragansett chiefs controlled some other groups besides their own tribe. Among these other tribes were the Nipmuck and Wampanoag.

Narragansett lands once covered most of what is Rhode Island, including the area west of Narragansett Bay (pictured).

The Narragansett may have been the largest and strongest tribe in New England when British people first came to the New World. The Narragansett were generous and friendly. When Puritan minister Roger Williams went to Rhode Island after he was forced to leave Massachusetts in 1636, he was warmly welcomed. The Narragansett gave him land. There, he established a settlement that later became the city of Providence. After other white settlers followed Williams, though, wars broke out between the whites and the Narragansett. In less than forty years, the Narragansett were almost completely wiped out.

This illustration shows Narragansett tribal members greeting Puritan minister Roger Williams.

HISTORY

Early contact with Europeans

American Indians lived in what is now the northeastern United States by the end of the last Ice Age. That was around 11,000 B.C. They were wanderers who hunted large mammals. When the great ice caps melted, the Arctic mammals died or moved farther north. The Indians had to change the way they lived. The people who settled by the coast and waterways of New England between 10,000 and 700 B.C. were the ancestors of the Narragansett.

Italian explorer Giovanni da Verrazano went to the area in 1524. He stayed with the Narragansett for fifteen days. He wrote, "The people have the most civil customs that we have found on this voyage. . . . Their manner is sweet and gentle." Over the next century, Europeans had more and more

Italian explorer Giovanni da Verrazano was one of the first explorers to make contact with the Narragansett.

Early European settlers traded iron goods with the Narragansett.

1914–1918
WWI is fought in Europe

1929
Stock market crash begins the Great Depression

1941
Bombing at Pearl Harbor forces United States into WWII

1945
WWII ends

1950s
Reservations no longer controlled by federal government

1983
The U.S. government officially recognizes the Narragansett tribe

contact with the Narragansett. Most often, relations were friendly.

Some Europeans came to Rhode Island because the nearby waters offered some of the best fishing in the world. The Europeans brought with them goods made of iron that they traded with the tribe. They also brought new diseases, such as smallpox and plague, to which the native people were not immune. The Narragansett escaped some of the worst epidemics, which killed off most of the Wampanoag and other tribes. The members of these tribes who survived the epidemics joined the Narragansett. This made the tribe even stronger than it had been before.

Settlers come and wars follow

The Narragansett welcomed Puritan minister Roger Williams to Rhode Island. Williams spoke out against European colonists who took land from the Native Americans.

In 1636, the Massachusetts Bay Colony forced Puritan minister Roger Williams and a few of his followers to leave. Colonial officials were upset because Williams said it was wrong to take Indian lands by force. He also said that people should not be punished because they had different religious beliefs. Narragansett chief Miantonomi had heard of Williams. He welcomed the minister and his followers, and gave them a place to build homes.

Over the next forty years, the Narragansett often fought wars with other tribes as they tried to hold on to their power over New England. They also had to deal with more and more British settlers. In 1675, the United Colonies of New England began King Philip's War against the Wampanoag. They also declared war on the Narragansett because Narragansett chief Canonchet would not give up Wampanoag people who had fled from the war.

European colonists fought the Narragansett because they aided the Wampanoag tribe during King Philip's War in 1675.

On December 16, 1675, the colonial army attacked a Narragansett fort. This event came to be called the Great Swamp Fight. One person who took part in the battle said that between six hundred and one thousand Narragansett warriors died. The warriors' families were then hunted down and brutally treated. By the time the war came to an end in the summer of 1676, perhaps only two hundred Narragansett were still alive.

Survivors on the reservation

Of the Narragansett who were left, some were made slaves. Others joined the Niantic, a related tribe. The combined group took the name Narragansett. They lived as a small independent unit on a 64-square-mile reservation in southern New England for more than two hundred years. In 1880, however, the Rhode Island legislature bought the reservation. The government hoped this would make the tribe break up. Even after this, the Narragansett were able to stay together as a community. In the 1920s, they began a long struggle to win back their lands.

In 1978, the Narragansett won a lawsuit against the state of Rhode Island for the return of some of their traditional lands. In 1983, the Narragansett won recognition from the U.S. government. Federally recognized tribes have official relations with the U.S.

Some Native Americans were forced into slavery after they were defeated in battle.

government. Without federal recognition, the tribe does not exist in the eyes of the government. This kind of tribe does not get financial or other help.

Religion

The Narragansett believed in a creator god called Cautantowwit. He made the first people from stone.

The crow was a god in the Narragansett religion.

Then, he smashed them and created the ancestors of all other people. The Narragansett also believed in a spirit called Chepi, who was descended from the souls of the dead. Trained healers often called upon his power. Chepi was feared because he could punish people who did not behave in the right way. He might make them get sick or even cause them to die. Chepi warned Indians who followed the English lifestyle that bad things would happen if they did not go back to a traditional Indian way of life.

The Narragansett also had many lesser gods and spirits. One of these was the crow, who gave them corn and beans—their main crops—after he stole them from Cautantowwit's garden.

Many Indians in southern New England thought that strange or outstanding events were the work of the god Manittoo. This belief made some tribes think that the white people who came to Narragansett were gods. That was because they brought unfamiliar tools and ways, as well as printing and writing. The fact that they were viewed as gods often made it easy for the English colonists to have friendly relations with the Narragansett.

Government

The Narragansett were led by lesser chiefs called sachems (pronounced *SAY-chums*). These leaders were under the command of a grand sachem, who

Pessacus

Canonicus

Mixanno

Canonicus

Symbols such as these were used to identify sachems, a type of Narragansett chief. Sachems still serve in tribal government.

lived in the tribe's largest village. The grand sachem title was hereditary (handed down to relatives). Often, a sachem shared power with another person. The most popular arrangement was for a sachem to share power with a nephew. When there was no close male relatives to share the title, a female relative might become sachem.

The sachems made sure that all members of the tribe had enough land to take care of themselves. For their services, the sachems were paid in deerskins, corn, and other food. If a family did not like the way a sachem ran the tribe, it could simply join another tribe. It was viewed as a matter of pride and wealth for a sachem to have a large number of subjects. As a result, sachems were careful to treat their people well.

In the 18th century, as it took over the tribe's lands, the Rhode Island government tried to outlaw the position of sachem. The Narragansett ignored this. They still followed their sachems and a tribal council.

At the beginning of the 20th century, the U.S. government saw the Narragansett tribe as extinct. In 1983, however, the remaining Narragansett people were recognized by the federal government. Today, the tribal government is run by a nine-member elected tribal council. This council is led by a sachem and has five members. Also part of the

Sachem Matthew Thomas attended an April 2000 hearing at the
Rhode Island Statehouse.

council are a secretary and treasurer, as well as a medicine man or woman. The tribal government also has several departments, such as Housing and Finance.

Economy

The early Narragansett had many ways to get food. They not only farmed and fished, but also hunted and gathered.

When the Narragansett won recognition from the federal government in 1983, they were able to get government aid that they could use for public services, such as education and health care. The Narragansett set out to try to be self-sufficient.

Today, the tribal government employs more Narragansett than any other business or service. About three dozen members of the tribe work for the tribal government. Others who are part of the reservation take care of a community garden or harvest trees. Some also work in the building trades in towns near the reservation or work in the tourist trade. Among the tourist attractions in the area are the Dover Indian Trading Post in Rockville and the Narragansett Indian Longhouse, which gives lectures and tours for visitors.

This chimney was built by Narragansett stonemasons. Some Narragansett make a living practicing the traditional skill of using stone for building.

DAILY LIFE

Families

In Narragansett families, women gardened and cooked food.

To have fun, Narragansett men in early times liked to smoke and gossip. They played games, including a kind of football. They also threw dice and danced. Women, who grew and prepared most of the food, took pride in their interesting recipes.

Buildings

The Narragansett moved in both the winter and the summer. In the summer, they moved so they could plant and gather on good lands. In the winter, they moved to get to a warmer place where the hunting was good. Sometimes, they were forced to move when fleas and other biting insects became a problem or to get away from illnesses that sometimes struck their villages. Because the people moved so often, the Narragansett's wigwams had to be easy to take apart and put back together. They also had to be easy to carry. The roofs of wigwams were made of chestnut or birch bark attached to the top of bent poles that were stuck in the ground. In the winter, the people put mats or animal skins on the roof and floor to keep their homes warm. A hole in the roof let the smoke from the fire escape.

Two or more families might share one wigwam. The Narragansett also built shacks so that family members could sleep near their crops. This helped farmers protect young plants from birds and other predators.

In the 1940s, the Narragansett built a traditional longhouse on the reservation to serve as a community center. In the 1990s, plans were made to build a new community center as well as new homes on the reservation.

Seafood, including shellfish, was a food source for the coastal Narragansett.

Food

Before the Europeans destroyed the Narragansett culture, the natives ate many different kinds of food. Along the coast and in swamps and streams, women caught clams, oysters, and shellfish. In the woods, they found wild onions, strawberries, and other plants, depending on what was in season. Men got the fields ready, and women grew the crops. The main foods the Narragansett grew were corn, beans, and squash.

Men hunted many types of small and large game, including rabbits, squirrels, and bears. In the winter, they fished through the ice. Men also grew their own tobacco. To smoke it, they molded or carved special pipes. To smoke a peace pipe with another person was a way to show that a new friendship had begun.

Clothing

Little is known about the traditional clothing worn by the Narragansett. In summer, men most likely wore breechcloths. A breechcloth is a garment that

The Narragansett created beads like these and used them for trade.

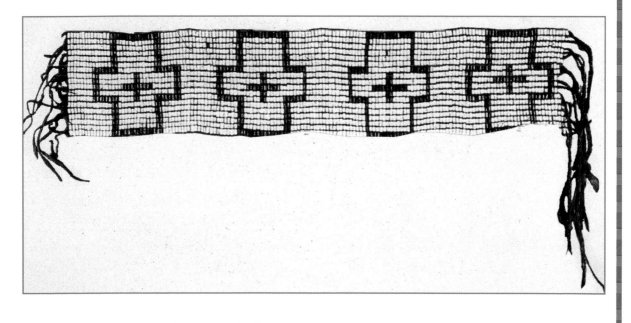

hangs from the waist and passes between the legs. Women wore leather or woven skirts. Beads were popular. Wampum—beads carved from the shells of local clams—were used both as decorations and in trade.

Healing practices

Narragansett healing practices went hand in hand with religion. People known as pawwaws (a word from which the term "powwow" comes) were in charge of religious and healing ceremonies. To gain their positions, pawwaws had to be able to contact the spirit world and to heal or injure other people. To show their power, a pawwaw might make magic arrows from the hair of an enemy. They might also cause a real arrowhead to hurt someone. Most often, pawwaws gave massages or laid on hands to cure the sick. Pawwaws were usually men. Women who knew how to make medicines from plants were called to help at the birth of a child.

Today, medicine men and women still play a big role in tribal life. In addition to the health care these healers provide, the reservation has an Indian Health Program that is run by the tribe. Visiting nurses also come to the reservation from hospitals in the Providence area.

Narragansett pawwaws were responsible for healing and religious ceremonies.

CUSTOMS

Marriage

Historians believe that three generations of two different Narragansett families would live together in one house. A woman probably moved in with her husband's family after she married.

A sachem would only marry a woman of high rank, such as the daughter of another sachem. Sometimes sachems had two or three wives if they could afford to support them.

Festivals

The Narragansett honored Cautantowwit, the creator, with a *nickommo*. In this special ceremony, the people burned or buried their most precious possessions as a sacrifice to the creator god. They also held a feast of thanksgiving for the god in the autumn. Some of the foods eaten at the feast were turkey, cranberries, and pumpkin pie.

Death and dying

Old men got the bodies of the dead ready for burial. First, they rubbed the bodies with mud or soot. Objects were then placed in the grave to go with

the soul to Cautantowwit's house. There, the
Narragansett believed the dead would live much
as they had on earth. Sometimes, a sick or dead
person's home was burned to prevent infection
or a visit from the evil spirit that had made the
person ill. A dead person's name was never
mentioned again.

Narragansett
tribe members
prepared for a
festival that
included
traditional
dancing.

Economic issues are an ongoing concern for the Narragansett. Tribe members attended a hearing in Washington, D.C., concerning the tribe's gambling rights.

Current tribal issues

The Narragansett today still strive for economic self-sufficiency. Housing projects have been designed to move elderly people and families to the reservation, where no one had lived before. A bingo parlor is also planned.

Sachem Miantonomi (standing, right) attempted to organize various tribes against the English colonists, but failed.

Notable People

The Narragansett sachem Miantonomi (d. 1643) was the first of his people to make friends with the English colonists. He was also one of the first American Indians to try to create an alliance of different tribes to oppose the whites. In a famous

Canonicus (standing, center) led the Narragansett against the English colonists during King Philip's War.

speech, he said: "These English having gotten our land, they with scythes cut down the grass, and their hogs spoil our clam banks, and we shall all be starved." Miantonomi could not get the many tribes to work together, however. He was put to death by the Mohegan tribe in 1643.

Other notable Narragansett include: Canonchet, who was Miantonomi's son and successor and a leader during King Philip's War (1675–1676); Canonicus, Miantonomi's uncle, who took care of matters within the tribe while Miantonomi dealt with problems outside the tribe; and Quaiapen, a female sachem and Canonicus's daughter-in-law, who led part of the tribe during King Philip's War.

For More Information

Algonquians of the East Coast. Alexandria, VA: Time-Life Books, 1995.

Beals, Carleton. *Colonial Rhode Island.* Camden, NJ: Thomas Nelson, 1970.

Simmons, William S. *The Narragansett.* New York: Chelsea House, 1989.

Summer Institute of Linguistics. *Living Languages of the Americas: United States of America.* http://www.sil.org/lla/usa_lg.html, March 7, 1997.

Through Indian Eyes: The Untold Story of Native American Peoples. Pleasantville, NY: Readers Digest, 1995.

Glossary

Ancestors dead relatives

Epidemic an outbreak of disease that affects many people

Puritan a member of a 16th- and 17th-century Protestant group in England and New England

Reservation a plot of land set aside by the U.S. government for Native Americans

Sachem a type of Narragansett chief

Sacrifice the act of offering something precious to a god

Treaty agreement

Tribe a group of people who live together in a community

Wampum beads used by Native Americans as decoration and as money

Index